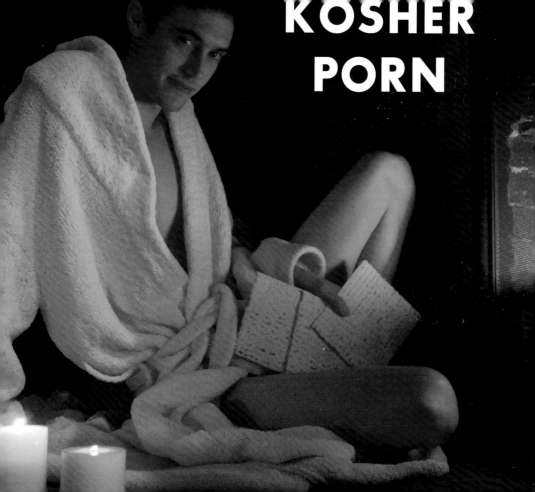

# KOSHER PORN

## SARAH ROSEN

#### PHOTOS BY
### TOM STOKES

### RUNNING PRESS
#### PHILADELPHIA · LONDON

Published by Running Press,
A Member of the Perseus Books Group

ISBN 978-0-7624-5655-0
Library of Congress Control Number: 2014942143

E-book ISBN 978-0-7624-5650-5

9  8  7  6  5  4  3  2  1
Digit on the right indicates the number of this printing

Cover and interior design by Josh McDonnell
Edited by Jordana Tusman
Typography: Akzidenz, Avenir, Helvetica, and Lato

Running Press Book Publishers
2300 Chestnut Street
Philadelphia, PA 19103-4371

Visit us on the web!
www.runningpress.com

To my parents, for being okay with this.

לדור ודור

# INTRODUCTION

Shalom! If you opened this book in search of pornography, I suggest that you quietly close the cover and turn to the Internet. But if Hebrew-speaking, challah-eating mensches turn you on, then MAZEL TOV! You're in the right place.

The blog behind this book, *Porn4Jews* (Porn4Jews.com), began after I had been living, and, more importantly, dating, in New York City for a year and a half after graduating from college. During that time, as I perused online dating sites and grabbed drinks with strangers I was set up with, I encountered many eligible bachelors who reaffirmed what I *wasn't* looking for in a match. But I also began to home in on the qualities that I *was* looking for. I liked the dark-haired smart ones who were family-oriented, seriously funny, and fully equipped to say the blessings at Shabbos dinner with my parents. What I liked was, in a word, Jewish.

So, I set out to celebrate my traditional, Bubbe-approved taste in romantic partners through a blog, in which Jewish values meet modern-day memes. This kind of "porn" is nudity-free, 100 percent kosher-certified, and, if we did our job right—pretty damn funny. In other words, this porn is marriage material.

We hope that the following pages will provide you with enough cute Jews spitting game to get you through a few bad JDates, a too-long Seder, or a low-key night at home with your laptop and some hummus. Hopefully, this book is also a fun way to brush up on your Judaism. You never know whom your newfound knowledge might impress. L'chaim!

MY GRANDPARENTS SAID YOU'RE
ALWAYS WELCOME FOR SHABBOS.

ASHKENAZIC ON THE STREET . . .

SEPHARDIC IN BED.

YOUR MOM GAVE ME HER KUGEL RECIPE

WE GO TOGETHER LIKE PASTRAMI AND RYE.

MY SHUL OR YOURS?

GIMMEL IS
FOR GADOL.

YOU'VE GOT A LULAV. I'VE GOT AN ETROG. LET'S GET SHAKIN'!

I'M FAMOUS FOR MY RUACH.

I'LL GLADLY TRY YOUR
FORBIDDEN FRUIT.

YOUR DAD AND I
AGREE ABOUT ISRAEL.

YOU ARE MY CHOSEN PERSON.

MY COUSIN'S WIFE'S
BROTHER IS IDAN RAICHEL.
I CAN GET US BACKSTAGE.

I KNOW
HOW TO KEEP
YOU SATISFIED.

I LOVE PURIM BECAUSE OF ITS STRONG FEMALE PROTAGONIST.

# HAPPY SUKKOT. TONIGHT WE'RE DOING IT UNDER THE STARS.

I WENT TO CAMP BEN-YEHUDA TOO!

WE'LL RAISE OUR KIDS
ON *SHALOM SESAME*.

# THEY'RE REAL.

# PHARAOH'S HEART ISN'T THE ONLY THING GOD HARDENED.

I'VE GOT ALL THE BEST MOVES.

I'M NOT AFRAID TO MAKE SOME NOISE.

DON'T MOVE.

I'LL BE RIGHT BACK AFTER I DAVEN.

PASS THE HORSERADISH.

I LIKE IT HOT.

JUST MEETING YOU MADE ME WANT TO BREAK A GLASS.

IT'S SHABBOS . . . HOW SHALL
WE AMUSE OURSELVES?

IF YOU'RE FREE LATER, THEY'RE SHOWING *SCHINDLER'S LIST* AT THE JCC.

I'LL BE YOUR
PROMISED LAND.

# TONIGHT'S A MEAT MEAL.

SHAVUA TOV.

LET'S GET SPICY.

I ALSO HAVE AN APARTMENT
IN JERUSALEM.

MY MATZOH BALLS ARE THE BEST IN TOWN.

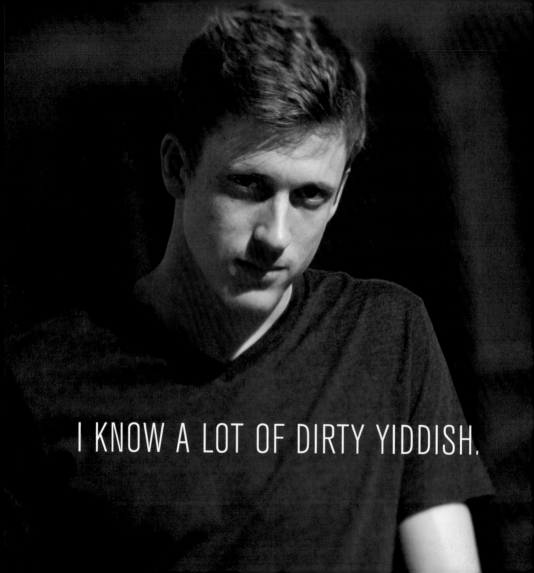

# WHO'S YOUR ABBA?

# I'LL SHOW YOU HOW A REAL SABRA DOES IT.

I KNOW OUR LOVE WILL LAST LONG DISTANCE. EVEN THOUGH WE ONLY MET LAST WEEK ON BIRTHRIGHT.

I GREW UP REFORM BUT I'D GO RECONSTRUCTIONIST FOR YOU.

I CAN GET A DISCOUNT ON ALL YOUR
FAVORITE DEAD SEA PRODUCTS.

# LET'S BE FRUITFUL AND MULTIPLY!

I COULDN'T HELP BUT CHECK
YOU OUT DURING KOL NIDRE.

I'M SO GLAD OUR THERAPISTS
INTRODUCED US.

# GUESS WHERE I HID THE AFIKOMEN?

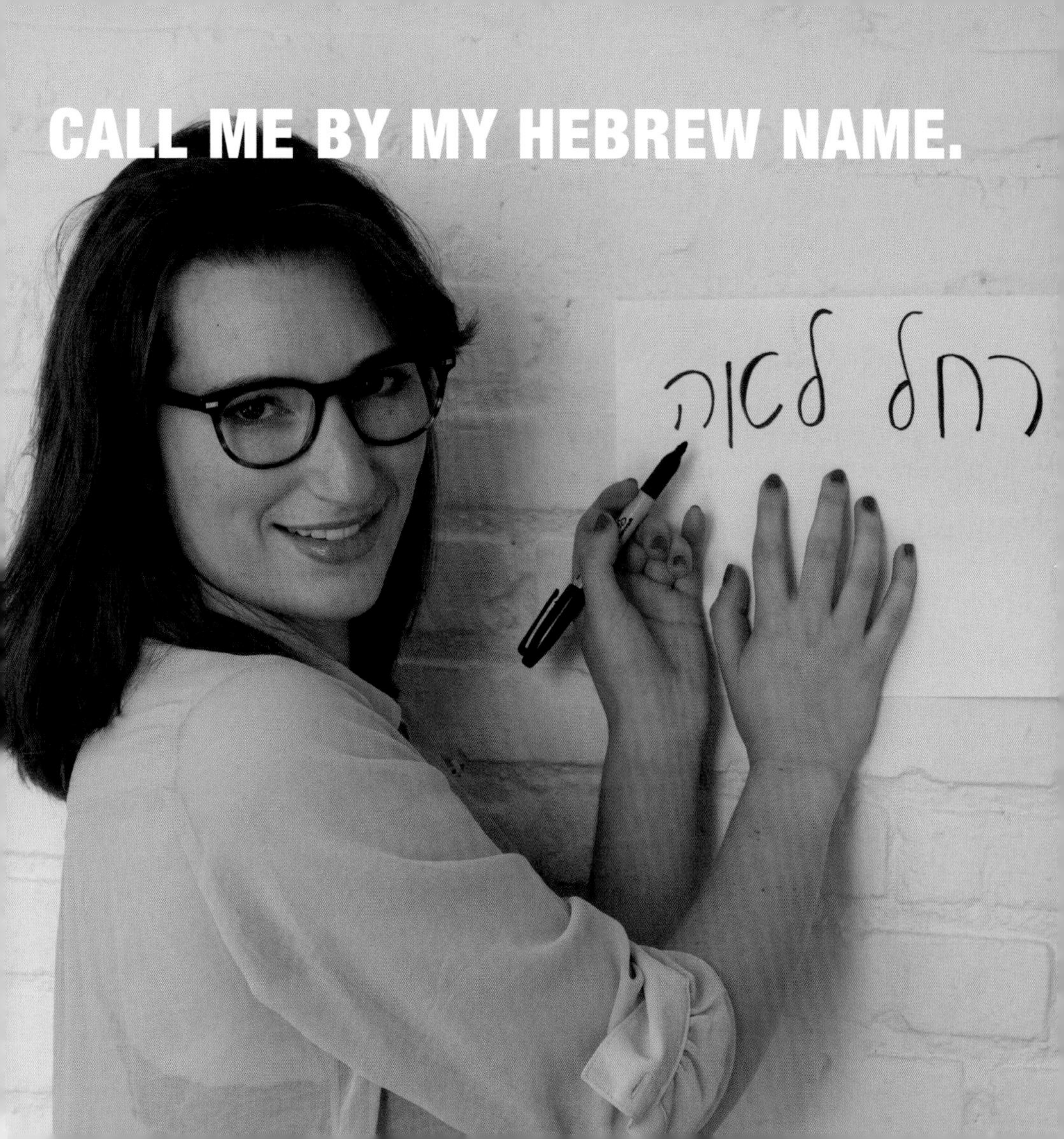
CALL ME BY MY HEBREW NAME.
רחל לבוה

MY IDEAL MÉNAGE À TROIS: YOU, ME, AND *SEINFELD*.

I WANT TO TASTE YOUR HAMANTASCHEN.

WHEN YOU'RE WITH ME
YOU WON'T NEED EL AL.

IT'S A MITZVAH IF WE DO IT ON SHABBOS.

I WANT TO KNOW YOU
LIKE ADAM KNEW EVE.

WE'LL ALWAYS HAVE BEN COHEN'S BAR MITZVAH.....

I CAN SCHMOOZE WITH
YOUR MESHUGINA UNCLE.

YOU KNOW WHAT I'M WISHING FOR.

# NEXT YEAR IN JERUSALEM?

## HOW ABOUT RIGHT HERE, RIGHT NOW.

BLUM. JAMES BLUM.

IT DOESN'T HAVE TO BE PURIM
FOR US TO PLAY DRESS-UP.

# I'D NEVER GET A TREE.

MEETING YOU WAS EVEN BETTER
THAN MY POST-YOM KIPPUR BAGEL.

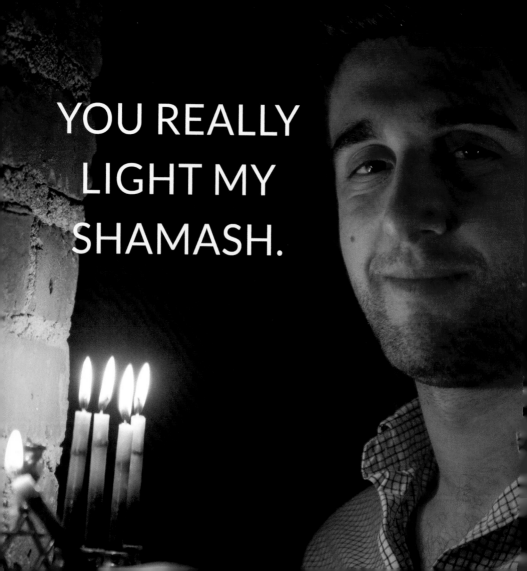

LET'S LEAVE THE DOOR
OPEN FOR ELIJAH.

# WE'LL SPEND A ROMANTIC WEEKEND
## . . . . AT MY BUBBE'S IN FLORIDA.

# I'M HALF-JEWISH

# ON MY MOTHER'S SIDE.

# I'LL LOVE YOU ALMOST AS MUCH AS YOUR MOM DOES.

I MADE SHAKSHUKA. WE NEED TO KEEP OUR STRENGTH UP.

# I ONLY KEEP IT KOSHER
# IN THE KITCHEN.

# YOUR SAFTA SAYS I SPEAK GREAT HEBREW.

LET'S MAKE SOME BABIES AND SEND
THEM ALL ON BIRTHRIGHT.

AS GOD COMMANDED . . .

GO DOWN, MOSES.

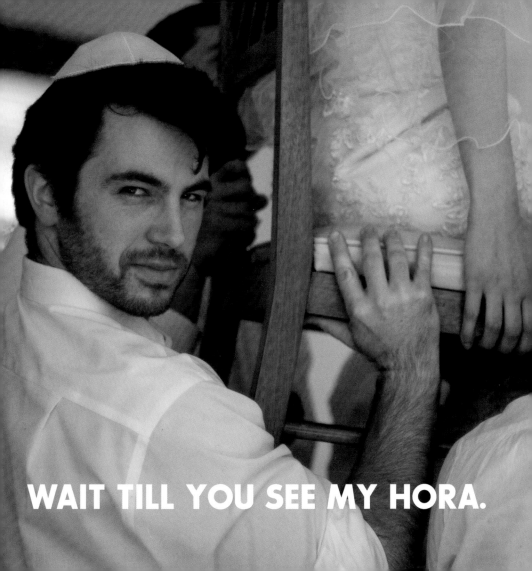

WAIT TILL YOU SEE MY HORA.

I'LL SCHMEAR
YOU WITH LOVE.

I'D MAKE ALIYAH FOR YOU.

LET'S PLANT ALL KINDS OF
SEEDS THIS TU B'SHEVAT.

MY BUBBE TAUGHT ME TO MAKE IT HOT AND STEAMY.

STICK WITH ME AND YOU CAN
EAT RICE EVERY PESACH.

I LIKE MY MEN LIKE I LIKE MY LATKES: HOT AND COVERED IN OIL.

# SO WILL I SEE YOU AT THE SHEVA BRACHOT?

JUST CALL ME THE LAND OF MILK AND HONEY.

LET'S GIVE OUR PARENTS
SOMETHING TO KVELL ABOUT.

ANYTHING YOU NEED, MY DAD KNOWS A GUY.

THIS PURIM, LET'S DRESS UP IN OUR BIRTHDAY SUITS.

IF OUR DESCENDANTS ARE GOING TO BE AS NUMEROUS AS THE STARS, WE'D BETTER GET STARTED.

# I'M A PAREVE DESSERT FOR ANY MEAL.

I PLAYED BASEBALL
AT BRANDEIS.

I CAN HOLD MY OWN AT YOUR FAMILY SEDER.

I'D DIP
MY APPLE
IN YOUR
HONEY.

I ALWAYS USE
PROTECTION.

# STAY THE NIGHT. I'LL MAKE YOU CHALLAH FRENCH TOAST IN THE MORNING.

HAD WE ONLY GONE TO FIRST BASE

. . . DAYENU!

I TOLD YOUR MOM
SHE CAN DELETE YOUR
JDATE PROFILE.

I'LL HAVE YOU SPEAKING HEBREW IN NO TIME

WANT TO COME UP? I HAVE *THE PRINCE OF EGYPT* ON NETFLIX.

I CAN'T BELIEVE WE HAD THE SAME TORAH PORTION!

**MY MEAT IS KOSHER.**

## ACKNOWLEDGMENTS

There are so many people to thank and these are just a few. I'd like to thank Myrsini Stephanides, Lydia Blyfield, Andrea Pass, Jordana Tusman, Josh McDonnell, Cassie Drumm, and everyone at Running Press and Perseus Books Group for their support and for making this book possible. To all of the models in New York, Israel, and New Haven: Meeting and working with you was the best part of this project. You made it what it is and I cannot thank you enough. You're always welcome for Shabbos.

I'd like to thank Barbara Davilman for her endless help; Doug Chernack and Rachel Kauder Nalebuff for their generosity and advice; Elisa Zuritsky for her wisdom, contributions, and encouragement; Julie Shain, Antoine Combelles, Hunter Wolk, Yael Zinkow, Ryan Kline, Drew Westphal, and Jenny Weber for their input and support; Adam King for his contributions, brilliance, and amazing attitude; the Ben-Atar and King families for their help, love, and community (this book would not exist without the shul group); Heddy and Rafi Stern for being the Rebbetzin and Rebbe of this project/my life (and for being my "inspiration," according to them); everyone who helped make our trip to Israel such a joy and such a success, especially Roma Ben-Atar and Oded Barr, and Adam Sagir for his wonderful support and for being the best tour guide imaginable; Bill Esper for his encouragement and for teaching me what it means to be an artist; Courtney Grafton and Amelie Peisl for being fantastic cheerleaders; Peter Mezan for teaching me how to be a businesswoman; all of the Porn4Jews readers around the world for the extended community; Dani Schoffman for so much, including his contributions, model-scouting, and constant help and feedback.

I'd especially like to thank my whole family for their support, love, and modeling. Big thanks to Annie Rosen for her smarts and encouragement. Barbara Goren and David Rosen, there are no words—thank you for everything. And, most importantly, I'd like to thank the brilliant and talented Tom Stokes, without whom this project would not exist—to many more collaborations!